ENGLAND

LANDMARKS, LANDSCAPES & HIDDEN TREASURES

Publisher and Creative Director: Nick Wells
Project Editor: Laura Bulbeck
Art Director: Mike Spender
Digital Design and Production: Chris Herbert

Special thanks to: Sara Robson, Frances Bodiam, Amanda Leigh, Victoria Lyle,
Julia Rolf, Gemma Walters, Polly Willis, Laura Zats and Taylor Steinberg.

FLAME TREE PUBLISHING

Crabtree Hall, Crabtree Lane
Fulham, London SW6 6TY
United Kingdom

www.flametreepublishing.com

First published 2015

15 17 19 18 16
1 3 5 7 9 10 8 6 4 2

A CIP record for this book is available from the British Library.

ISBN: 978 1 78361 421 9

Printed in Singapore

ENGLAND

LANDMARKS, LANDSCAPES & HIDDEN TREASURES

Tamsin Pickeral and Michael Kerrigan

FLAME TREE
PUBLISHING

Contents

Introduction

The pace of life beats fast in today's society; unwittingly the majority finds itself locked in the greater mechanisms, the vast, endlessly turning wheels of big business and tight schedules, juggling too many things with too few hands.

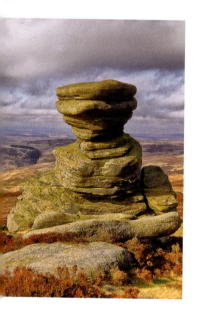

To take hold of the corporate heart and kill the insistent pulse of stress is to shake loose, throw off the bonds of restriction and step into a world of glorious scenery; a hidden treasure trove of inspirational landscape, the history of its past and the eminence of the nation – this is England at its very best and most spectacular. This wonderful collection of photographs of some of the famous and not so famous corners of England offers a glimpse of the sedate, the quiet, and the idyllic, a respite from the loud cacophony of everyday life. Here England of both the past and present is captured by the keen eye of the photographic artist in a series of evocative shots.

When travelling to the North you will find the industrial heart of the country; yet northern England retains much of its original beauty – it is easy to look beyond the aesthetic blight of industrialism and see the treasure beneath. The coal mines of Sheffield, the ship-building along the banks of the River Tyne, and the iron works – all this, and yet this region is also home to the beautiful North York Moors and the scenic Pennines, England's spine of hills running from Derbyshire to Northumberland. The Yorkshire area bears industry as a necessary evil, but the town of York, with her inspiring York Minster, wipes it clean. Newcastle-upon-Tyne is a northern captain of industry but also one of the best examples of Victorian town planning; she now welcomes the weary traveller with the stunning image of a bronze angel, set high on a hill above Tyneside.

The North-West offers you Cumbria which is home to some truly breath taking views. A place often noted for its stunning mountains, valleys and serene flowing waters. Home to the highest point in England with Scafell Pike reaching up to 3,209 feet, this is an incredible location. Enrich your creative senses and stimulate your artistic side, as Cumbria has the capability to leave you feeling inspired and refreshed. Its natural beauty serves as a nice break from the hustle of metropolitan life, as it is one of the most sparsely populated areas within England. You'll also find towns such as Blackpool, a vibrant and thriving place, home of the tower that warmly welcomes its holidaymakers from miles around with an exhilarating beacon. With an array of small towns and villages, Cheshire is a county of agricultural history. This rural location has a multitude of elements to offer its visitors. Its Roman heritage is particularly on display in Chester's city walls and Roman gardens. With tranquil winding rivers you will find that this scenic county has plenty to offer.

Travel south and soon the echoes of pre-history turn to the rhetoric of Shakespeare and the muted cry of long past battles. This is the 'cockpit of England', the 'heart of England' and the birthplace of the great Elizabethan playwright. Across the lands of the South Midlands battles were fought in the incessant struggle for power. This area is also the very middle of England; an ancient cross outside Coventry marks the spot. Within this remarkable area you will find Derbyshire, where a vast amount of the Peak District National Park resides. Each area within this region has its own distinctive character, the

mystical appeal of Nottinghamshire which housed the romantic hero and outlaw Robin Hood and his merry men is also home to some of the oldest trees in Europe. The heart of England is full of quaint limestone villages and tranquil rivers, but it is also home to enchanting cities such as Oxford, with its mesmerising spires rising across the skyline.

In East Anglia the flat landscape struggles against the battering North Sea, much of the country lying below sea level and formed from reclaimed land. The salt marshes, eerie carpets of sodden ground and resilient rushes, sway to the piping song of the oystercatcher and hide rare nesting birds. Here great towns have disappeared beneath the relentless sea; Dunwich, once a thriving port and the seat of the first East Anglican Christian Bishop in the sixth century, was swallowed by the waves; the ruins of churches are now a playground for fish. Here in East Anglia the agricultural landscapes, rural tranquillity of village greens and coastal scenes of beach huts combine with the beautiful architecture of the city of Cambridge, or the magnificent Lincoln Cathedral rising up from its limestone plateau. It is a place of remarkably unspoilt beauty.

Down towards London and the South-East: the manicured lawns of Buckinghamshire, Berkshire and Surrey, beech woods of golden yellow, soft swelling green hills and the garden county – Kent. This is a gentle countryside of quiet beauty and ripe, productive farm land, fruit and hops, conical oast houses unique in form and appeal. A quiet belt of semi-rural respite from the loud hammering of England's largest and most famous city – London. Bright lights, fast business, retail, commerce, entertainment, music and laughter – London is host to a seething energy, a stream of movement, conscious thought and consequential actions, but also boasts some of the most magnificent architectural buildings of history and of the future. As with so much of England, London was established by the Romans, who have left their mark from one end of the country to the other. Their planning, building and development shaped the country, her cities, roads and history of trading. They trod paths that had been worn

before them by man's ancestors and laid the foundations for future peoples. London loves to look back and cherish its great history, but also to look ahead with its ever changing skyline and its vibrant culture.

The great white cliffs of Dover on the south-east coast – synonymous with England and long the romantic subject of artists, poets and writers – gleam against the sea, a stalwart barricade looking towards the coast of France some 21 miles (34 km) away. This region has a multitude of factors to offer, with Brighton and Sussex in such close proximity, the list of possibilities appears to be infinite. Brighton Royal Pavilion with its extravagant oriental appearance is just moments away from the thriving city centre, where you can choose from a range of unique restaurants and shops whilst you navigate your way through the winding cobbled lanes. The New Forest located in Hampshire provides you with soft rolling hills and picturesque landscapes that are beautiful to behold.

Now down to England's boot – Cornwall, Devon and Somerset. The south-west counties are a world apart: here the climate is warmer, the terrain open moors, forests and rolling hills. The coastline is ragged, picturesque, beaten by the Atlantic, moulded, shaped and eaten away to great chunks of jagged rocks; surprising bays of sandy beaches are tucked amongst the granite headlands. The rugged nature of the Bedruthan Steps in Cornwall are enough to astound any traveller, this area of legend and mystery is like something from a fairytale. Devon's smooth beaches are the perfect place to relax and unwind, whilst the crashing waves contribute to defining a surfer's paradise. It is home to so many quaint towns where you can admire the charming scenery and choose from a selection of cafes for a traditional English cream tea. Creeping out of the boot and in an easterly direction, the character again changes. The sweeping plains of Salisbury, the magnificent New Forest, Dorchester and Thomas Hardy country, and on into Hampshire, home of the great naval base Portsmouth. England's indomitable antiquity is central to her fabric and Wiltshire is host to swirling mists of pre-history, the great white chalk horses, Stonehenge, Avebury, Silbury Hill; silent spectators on our present times, their secrets held tight.

Today England is a place as rich and diverse in culture, history and landscape as any. Every corner, secret or otherwise, of this small country has something to offer; a visual feast of colour, landscape and atmosphere. From a splash of bright sun shining on water, green trees reflected, to the soaring spire of a Gothic cathedral, pearly white, uplifting, a feat of manpowered engineering; from a crumbling castle, proud with the memories of once-great walls, to silent, watchful, strange stones from pre-history; there is no single defining characteristic for England, she is the finished masterpiece, a canvas of many different brushstrokes. May the road rise to meet you.

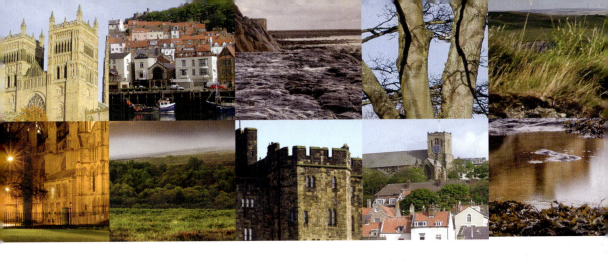

North-East England

Stretching from Northumbria, nestled against the Scottish border, to Sheffield, knocking on the door of the Midlands, this corridor of land forms the indomitable North-East of England.

Some two thousand years ago, the Romans moved in and claimed some of the most productive and wildly beautiful landscape in Britain. Today, Hadrian's Wall, the most impressive of Britain's Roman relics, snakes in ruins across the undulating backbone of the land, an ancient barricade and a reminder of the turbulent and bloody past played out on the windswept reaches of the North.

Bordered to the west by the Pennines, the North-East is home to a highly dramatic landscape that makes it one of the most popular destinations for hikers, birdwatchers and those seeking solitude. This part of England is rich in the ruined monuments of times and people past. Great castles such as Castle Howard and Lindisfarne Castle loom through rolling mists, while the shimmering skeletons of ancient buildings pepper the haunting landscape. The North-East is a landscape of exhilarating space, from the stalwart peaks of the Pennines and the roll of the North York Moors to the sweeping moorlands of heather, home to grouse and the wheeling curlew.

Lindisfarne Castle

NORTHUMBERLAND

Right. Lindisfarne Castle stands sentry over its small kingdom of Holy Island. The castle was built in 1549 using stones from the skeleton of the nearby ruined abbey, and was designed as a fortress against the marauding Scots and their allies the French. By the 1900s the castle had fallen into ruin, and in 1902 it was bought by Edward Hudson, founder of *Country Life* magazine. He commissioned the architect Sir Edwin Lutyens to restore the castle and in 1968 it was taken over and preserved by the National Trust.

Hadrian's Wall

NORTHUMBERLAND

Next page. Built around AD 120 at the order of the Roman Emperor Hadrian, this impressive barricade snaked its way for 73 miles (117 km) from Wallsend-on-Tyne to the Soloway Firth. The wall was a fantastic feat of engineering, constructed of stone in the eastern part and turf to the west, with a sophisticated system of defensive ditches running its length. Not just a wall, the structure incorporated 17 large forts, smaller forts and watch towers and was garrisoned by infantry and cavalry. It remained in use until AD 383.

Alnwick Castle
NORTHUMBERLAND

Right. This impressive medieval castle sits on a twelfth-century site and has been home to the powerful Percys, Earls and Dukes of Northumberland since 1309. Through the Middle Ages Alnwick was partially ruined during bloody border warfare, and was not restored until the eighteenth century. Described by the current Duke of Northumberland as 'Windsor of the North', the castle now houses stunning state rooms with works by Canaletto, Titian and Van Dyck. Recently Alnwick has provided the backdrop for two of the popular *Harry Potter* films.

St Mary's Lighthouse
TYNE & WEAR

Next page. At low tide you can walk across the concrete causeway just visible beneath the water in the foreground here. The rocks beyond were long a hazard for coastal shipping. In medieval times, a monastery on St Mary's Island kept a light burning as a warning; the modern lighthouse was built in 1898. It was decommissioned in 1984 – rendered redundant by new navigational equipment – but its dazzling white tower remains an important landmark. It indicates the northern limit of Whitley Sands, which extend all the way down to Cullercoats at the southern end of Whitley Bay.

Angel of the North
TYNE & WEAR

Right. The evocative silhouette of the Angel of the North rising from her hillside site, welcoming you to Tyneside, is a compelling mixture of ancient mysticism and modernism. The Angel herself is a celebration of clean line and simple, monumental form; the site a reclaimed former colliery pit. She was designed by the visionary contemporary artist Antony Gormley OBE and was unveiled in 1998. At 65 feet (20 m) high, and with a 177-foot (54-m) wingspan, she is thought to be the largest angel sculpture in the world.

Tyne Bridge
TYNE & WEAR

Next page. Newcastle-upon-Tyne grew from humble beginnings; first serving as an outpost for the Romans, it has continued to develop and is now the capital of the North. Despite massive industrial expansion, this great city remains one of the most attractive of northern cities, due in large part to the town planning of Victorian architect John Dobson. Newcastle is a city of bridges, with five historic and beautiful bridges spanning the Tyne; each different but magnificent, they are an inspiring gateway to the heart of the city.

Durham Cathedral
COUNTY DURHAM

Right. 'Grey towers of Durham yet well I love thy mixed and massive piles, half church of God, half castle 'gainst the Scot': the words of Sir Walter Scott, inscribed on a plaque on the Prebends Bridge overlooking the magnificent Durham Cathedral. William de St Carileph commissioned the Norman cathedral in 1093, building it on the site of an existing Saxon church. The cathedral sits on its rocky site, surrounded on three sides by the River Wear, and next to the great Durham Castle, which dates back to *c*. 1070.

North York Moors
YORKSHIRE

Next page. Far in the distance shimmers the village of Goathland, across miles of wide-open Yorkshire Moors. This is a place of myth and legend, superstition and great tales, a barren, rugged landscape of adventure and history. The Moors are crossed by the Cleveland Way and the Lyke Wake Walk, two long trails that wind through many miles of stunning countryside, historical sites and abundant wildlife. This wild country was the birthplace of Captain James Cook, one of the greatest explorers of all time.

Scarborough Harbour
YORKSHIRE

Right. Scarborough is still a working fishing port, though the industry has taken a hammering in recent years. Tourism has become increasingly crucial to the town. Fortunately, it has much to recommend it to the visitor: a stunning setting; a thousand-year history; and, in the Grand, one of the most handsome Victorian hotels in the British Isles. Of late, Scarborough has become a cultural centre: many artists, designers, filmmakers and writers are established here, whilst playwright Alan Ayckbourn even has his own theatre in the town.

Harrogate
YORKSHIRE

Next page. Springtime in Harrogate erupts in colour: this elegant Yorkshire spa town has long been noted for the riot of floral displays adorning just about every open space. The mineral spring here was discovered in the sixteenth century, but it was not until the 1890s that Harrogate reached its zenith as a health resort. Hence the Victorian vintage of its finest architecture: the Kursaal or Royal Hall theatre; the Royal Pump Room; the Majestic Hotel and the Westminster Arcades. Each year in summer, Harrogate hosts the Great Yorkshire Show.

York Minster
YORKSHIRE

Right. York is one of the most beautiful cities in Britain and is home to York Minster, the finest and largest of the Gothic cathedrals in Northern Europe. The Minster has an ancient, turbulent history, and has been destroyed and rebuilt since Roman times – remains of the Roman settlement on which the cathedral was built are visible in the undercroft. Next to the Minster is the fifteenth-century, half-timbered St William's College, originally home to the cathedral chantry priests.

Castle Howard
YORKSHIRE

Next page. The magnificent Castle Howard sits in a stately parkland setting; this is surely one of the most palatial of country seats. The house was designed in the early 1700s by the notable architect Sir John Vanbrugh and his assistant Nicholas Hawksmoor for the third Earl of Carlisle, and is home to an impressive collection of antique furniture. The grounds are as hauntingly beautiful as the house and include a circular mausoleum, designed by Hawksmoor, and the Temple of The Four Winds, designed by Vanbrugh.

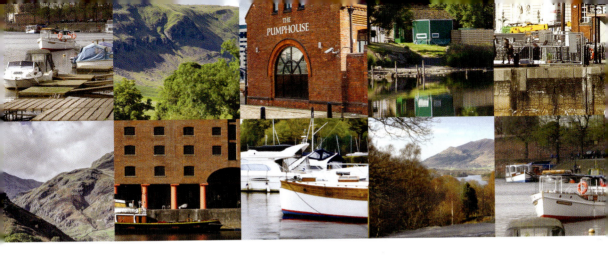

North-West England

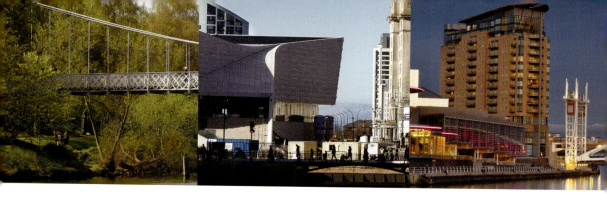

From the sublime splendour of Cumbria and the Lake District, through the romance of Lancashire and the cosmopolitan metropolis of Merseyside, to the ancient town of Chester, North-West England holds a uniquely diverse appeal.

Bordered by sea to the west, the rugged Pennine Mountains to the east, Scotland to the north and Wales to the south, the North-West is full of its own character and appeal. The Romans first settled the city that would become Chester in AD 79, fiercely guarding their fertile and productive new territory from the marauding Welsh. From these ancient

roots, the surrounding area emerged as a leader in industry, agriculture and tourism. Although the North-West is associated with cotton mills and coal mining, today it is also known for its astonishing landscape, which encompasses the wild, untamed glory of Cumbria and the majestic Lake Windermere.

The North-West is a place of extraordinary beauty, ranging from the soft, sandy coastlines of Cumbria to the rolling farmlands of the Cheshire Plains, from the tranquil lakes of Lancashire to the hubbub of Blackpool and her famous illuminations.

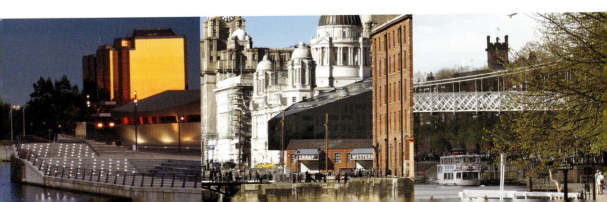

The Langdale Pikes
CUMBRIA

Right. In the heart of the Lake District is the Langdale Valley, a lush valley of green with sweeping views, topped by the imposing Langdale Pikes. These three rocky peaks are known as Pike of Stickle, Harrison Stickle and Pavey Ark. This is the country of mountains, valleys and water, and although the Langdale Pikes are smaller than some of their neighbours, they are just as impressive. Seen here from Copt Howe, the Langdale Pikes can also be viewed from across Lake Windermere, which is itself magnificent.

Lake Windermere
CUMBRIA

Next page. The huge Lake Windermere cuts a watery slash through the Lake District; to the west lies Grizedale Forest Park and to the east an expanse of beautiful country leading down towards the town of Kendal. On the southern shores of Windermere is Fell Foot Park, a pretty Victorian park with manicured gardens and fantastic views across the lake. Boating and recreation is primary here; this is a place to relax, unwind, and enjoy a gentle day's sailing, savouring the spectacular views across Lake Windermere.

Ashness Bridge
CUMBRIA

Right. Ashness Bridge, or the Old Packhorse Bridge, spans a riotous brook that wends its way towards the impressive Derwentwater. In the distance, the imposing craggy peaks of Skiddaw scowl down on the landscape, throwing a shadow across Keswick to the east, Bassenthwaite Lake to the west and Derwentwater to the south. The weary traveller of old stepping across Ashness Bridge has been replaced by the enthusiastic tourist; this has become a very popular trail, and is a beautiful scene at any time of the year.

Ullswater
CUMBRIA

Next page. William Wordsworth, wrote when describing, Ullswater that it was 'the happiest combination of beauty and grandeur, that any of the lakes affords'. This lake, in the north-east corner of the Lake District, is the second longest lake in the area, and snakes its way through the most dramatic scenery of great fells, woods and a ring of mountains at its southern end. The lake has attracted settlers for centuries, and takes its name from an early Norse settler, L'Ulf.

Blackpool Tower
LANCASHIRE

Right. Soaring 518 feet (158 m) into the air, Lancashire's Blackpool Tower dominates the miles of promenade. It is even more spectacular at night, when the tower forms part of the famous Blackpool Illuminations; it glows in the darkness, an elegant but opulent beacon of entertainment. The tower was begun in 1891 and is typical of the Victorian style of measured extravagance. At that time Blackpool was fast becoming one of the most popular seaside resort towns, a position that it has held for over 100 years.

Salford Quays
MANCHESTER

Next page. The sun sets over Salford Quays, casting an eerie light over the graceful footbridge that carries art-lovers across the Manchester Ship Canal to The Lowry. Thanks to this waterway, Salford was for many years one of Britain's most successful ports – despite being a good 45 miles (70 km) from the sea. In the post-war period, Salford saw hard times as traffic through the port fell away precipitously and by the 1970s this whole area was derelict. Its redevelopment from the 1980s was a pioneering example of urban regeneration.

The Pumphouse Inn
MERSEYSIDE

Right. The Albert Dock has been turned into a conservation area to preserve the fascinating history of Liverpool's emergence as a major port. The fortunes of the city are intrinsically bound to the development of her docks; it was the advent of the steamship in the 1840s that really saw Liverpool's trading take off. The Pumphouse Inn was built around 1878 and served as the pump house for the docks. It has since been converted to a pub, but retains some of its original character.

Albert Dock
MERSEYSIDE

Next page. Liverpool's Albert Dock is a testament to the powers of restoration and commercialism in the current climate of cultural and economic interest. The docks were officially opened in 1846 and were a huge achievement in the history of dock engineering. Liverpool's flourishing trading importance saw the docks filled with precious cargoes from all over the world. By 1972 shipping here had diminished and the docks were closed. After a massive restoration process the site has been turned into a thriving cosmopolitan centre of entertainment and cultural heritage.

Roman Gardens
CHESHIRE

Right. The Romans first established their camp of Deva on the site of modern Chester in AD 79, and set about construction of the monumental enclosing wall in an effort to keep the marauding Welsh at bay. This public area called The Roman Gardens was created in order to show off beautiful fragments from this camp, discovered during nineteenth century excavations, and include such sites as the baths and legionary headquarters. The Roman city wall that runs next to the gardens is one of the best surviving examples of Roman ramparts.

River Dee
CHESHIRE

Next page. The River Dee winds its way past the ancient scenic city of Chester, heading out towards the Irish Sea. The wide, blue ribbon passing Chester is spanned by many bridges, but only one footbridge – the elegant white Queen's Park Suspension Bridge. The bridge was originally built in 1852 in conj:unction with a development of city suburbs across the river. In 1922 the bridge was demolished and a new bridge was built to the designs of Charles Greenwood. The new bridge was expertly restored in 1998.

Heart of England

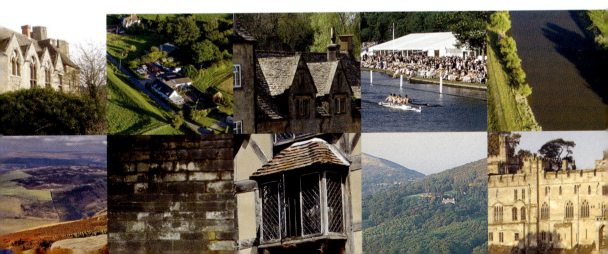

The Heart of England beats to a differing rhythm; the slow pastoral march of Herefordshire and Worcestershire, the thunder of Gloucestershire with her horseracing and eventing, the measured toll of Shakespeare's land, Warwickshire, the academic pulse of Oxfordshire and her lovely stone architecture, the hammer of industry through the West Midlands and the slow, easy tempo of beautiful Derbyshire, Nottinghamshire and Shropshire.

This middle England encompasses landscapes as wild and divergent as the histories played out here. To the north sits the rugged face of the Peak District, to the south the

impressive Cotswold Hills, their quaint limestone villages tucked into lush green farmland, behind mellow stone walls. Herefordshire, the land of the cider apple and the famous Hereford cow, rests in the shadow of the Welsh mountains to the west, while Oxford with her yellowed stone buildings and the tumbling River Cherwell, looks east.

Through England's heart winds a stream of steady waters, for this is an area rich in rivers and the birthplace of the great River Thames. Sparkling waters flowing through a verdant landscape, cattle and sheep grazing, houses set round a village green and traditional pubs – as diverse as this area's landscape is, it remains quintessentially, beautifully British.

Monsal Dale
DERBYSHIRE

Right. Right in the heart of Britain lies the Peak District, 540 square miles (1,398 square km) of uninterrupted glorious country, and Britain's first National Park. Sweeping away as far as the eye can see is the lush green of this fertile landscape of Monsal Dale, as viewed from Monsal Head. This small, stone farm nestled into the hillside is typical of the region: picturesque, at one with the scenery and a busy pocket of rural life.

The Salt Cellar
DERWENT EDGE, DERBYSHIRE

Next page. Wind, rain, ice and frost crafted this sculpture in stone over countless millennia: it is called the Salt Cellar on account of its distinctive shape. The millstone grit, which is characteristic of this part of the Peak District, is rough to the touch but comparatively soft and easily eroded: many weird and wonderful formations may be seen. In the valley in the background we see the blue waters of the Ladybower Reservoir and the Forestry Commission plantation on its southern side. The walk along Derwent Edge offers some of England's finest views.

Robin Hood Statue

NOTTINGHAMSHIRE

Right. Robin Hood is one of the most enduring and traditional of the 'people's heroes', and also one of the most mystical. The tales of Robin Hood cross over between fact and fiction; some ballads claim that he lived in Sherwood Forest, some in Yorkshire's Barnsdale Forest. Through all the stories Robin retains his chivalry, dignity and grace, battling the rich on behalf of the poor and hounding the Sheriff of Nottingham. James Woodford's statue outside Nottingham Castle perfectly captures the brave character of Britain's favourite outlaw.

Sherwood Forest

NOTTINGHAMSHIRE

Next page. In the north-east of Nottinghamshire lie the remains of Sherwood Forest, the one-time magnificent royal hunting grounds thought to have been established by William the Conqueror. Sherwood is, however, better known for its association with the famous folk hero Robin Hood. The great oak trees of the forest provided Robin and his merry men with shelter and protection from the wicked Sheriff of Nottingham. The forest is home to a great variety of plants and wildlife, such as the beautiful silver birch trees seen here.

Stokesay Castle
SHROPSHIRE

Right. This fine manor house dates back to the twelfth century, the gabled half-timbering on the north tower added on later during the sixteenth century. Stokesay has one of the best and oldest-surviving examples of a great hall; the scene surely of feisty banquets, the air spiced with savoury smells, wood-smoke, roasting meat and warm bodies round the roaring fireplace. The house was built by Lawrence of Ludlow, a prosperous wool merchant, and was later fortified by the de Sayes family, from whom it takes its name.

Hereford Cathedral
HEREFORDSHIRE

Next page. Standing serenely on the banks of the River Wye, Hereford Cathedral is a feast for the eyes. It is not only the predominantly Norman exterior that is so compelling, but also the interior, stunningly restored and home to two of Britain's greatest historic treasures; the Mappa Mundi, a medieval map of the world, is one of the finest ancient maps in Europe, and was painted by Richard of Haldingham around 1275, while the seventeenth-century Chained Library is the largest library of its kind in the world.

Symonds Yat
HEREFORDSHIRE

Right. The River Wye winds through the Forest of Dean, a picture of peace and tranquillity, but appearances can be deceptive here. When the river is in flood, it becomes a raging torrent: the deep gorge through which it flows so calmly was carved out by the spate over many centuries. Downstream of this spot, there are challenging rapids, a major draw for kayakers and white-water rafters. What makes this view is the vantage-point: Symonds Yat Rock rises a sheer 120 m (390 ft) above the river, affording panoramic vistas of the valley.

Malvern Hills
WORCESTERSHIRE

Next page. The Malvern Hills rest on the western boundary of Worcestershire, commanding views across Gloucestershire, Worcestershire and Herefordshire. They roll across the country for about eight miles (13 km); soft, green and pastoral, they offer some of the best walks for hiking enthusiasts. At nearly 1,400 feet (427 m) Worcestershire Beacon is the highest point, with British Camp, the Iron-Age hill fort, a slightly lower hill. From here there are stunning views across the patchwork countryside of Worcestershire, stretching as far as the eye can see.

The Old Bull
WORCESTERSHIRE

Right. This must be one of Britain's best known and loved inns, at least for fans of Radio Four's *The Archers*. The charming, timber-framed building was the model for the Bull at Ambridge in *The Archers* serial; the pub sign features an irritable-looking Hereford. The Old Bull has a long history of its own, however, and in 1582 Shakespeare stayed there on his way to collect his marriage certificate in Worcester. The village of Inkberrow is a suitably historic backdrop to the Old Bull.

Anne Hathaway's Cottage
WARWICKSHIRE

Next page. This charming thatched home, located near Stratford-Upon-Avon, is the quintessential English country cottage. Flowers bursting with colour, birds singing, the smell of summer; the perfect place for William Shakespeare to court his future wife, Anne Hathaway. One can only wonder what poetic words of romance the young playwright used, words he perhaps drew on again for his plays. The couple were married in 1582 in the village of Temple Grafton, and shortly afterwards moved into Shakespeare's father's house in Stratford-Upon-Avon. Six months after their wedding, Anne produced their first child, Susanna.

Shakespeare's Birthplace

WARWICKSHIRE

Right. It is extraordinary that, over 400 years after his birth, William Shakespeare still holds the position of one of the most highly regarded playwrights of all time. This great contributor to the history of literature was born in Stratford-upon-Avon, in this pretty, half-timbered house in Henley Street in 1564. From here Shakespeare's father, John, ran his successful business as a glove-maker and wool-dealer, eventually expanding the house to incorporate Joan Hart's Cottage, a single-bay building built on to the north-west end.

Warwick Castle

WARWICKSHIRE

Next page. Follow the River Avon around a bend and there, suddenly, is the breathtaking Warwick Castle, its reflection rippling on the surface of the water. An imposing vision of medieval splendour, the castle harbours a bloody and turbulent past, the scene of treachery and torture; a not unfamiliar history for Britain's great fortresses. Much of the interior was rebuilt during the seventeenth century, and then again in 1770 following a devastating fire. The grand exterior of the castle is matched by the handsome landscaped gardens, designed by the famous Capability Brown.

Tewkesbury Abbey
GLOUCESTERSHIRE

Right. The magnificent Tewkesbury Abbey dates back to the early twelfth century, and houses more medieval tombs than any other church in the country, with the exception of Westminster Abbey. According to notes by Shakespeare, one of the tombs holds the body of George, Duke of Clarence, who allegedly drowned in a butt of Malmsey wine! The abbey also has an impressive Norman tower that soars 132 feet (40 m) into the sky, and an outstanding Norman arch of six orders on the west front.

River Severn
GLOUCESTERSHIRE

Next page. The simple but charming timbered cottage, with white-painted plaster or brickwork, is perhaps most evocative of the British country home. Here, standing serenely along the banks of the slow-moving River Severn, one of Britain's longest and most impressive rivers, these quaint cottages are picture-perfect, right down to their reflected facades. This is a Britain that is hard to beat; the sun shines, there is not a breath of wind and even the river seems still, all bound in a pervading trance of quiet and tranquillity.

Snowshill
GLOUCESTERSHIRE

Right. The honeyed tones of Cotswold limestone, rolling green hills and riotous flowers make this area a visual delight. The small village of Snowshill is unspoilt and charming; small mellow houses crouch together, unpretentious yet beautiful in the simplicity of their design. A flash of bright sun, a gentle breeze and singing birds make this place a private Elysium. Two miles (3.2 km) outside the village is the Tudor Snowshill Manor, an eerie place of ghosts and history that adds to the slightly mysterious flavour of the village.

Oxford Spires
OXFORDSHIRE

Next page. With her majestic stone buildings and history steeped in refinement and academia, Oxford remains one of the jewels of Britain. The dreaming spires of the university's colleges soar skywards in a panorama as uplifting and lofty as the institution they enclose. The lively voice of debate, religious, political and cultural, echoes through the stones of her streets. Oxford, although now a fast-paced student town of shops, pubs and social activity, remains at her core entirely integral to the university, her history and culture shaped through the pursuit of knowledge.

Henley Regatta

OXFORDSHIRE

Right. A short stretch of the River Thames is home to the greatest, oldest and most famous river regatta in the world. Henley Royal Regatta was first held in 1839, and has taken place annually except during the First and Second World Wars. The race starts at Temple Island, home to James Wyatt's 1771 folly, and finishes a gruelling seven minutes later at Poplar Point. This is spectator sport, and the Henley enclosure is famous for its strict dress codes, champagne, Pimms, and strawberries with cream.

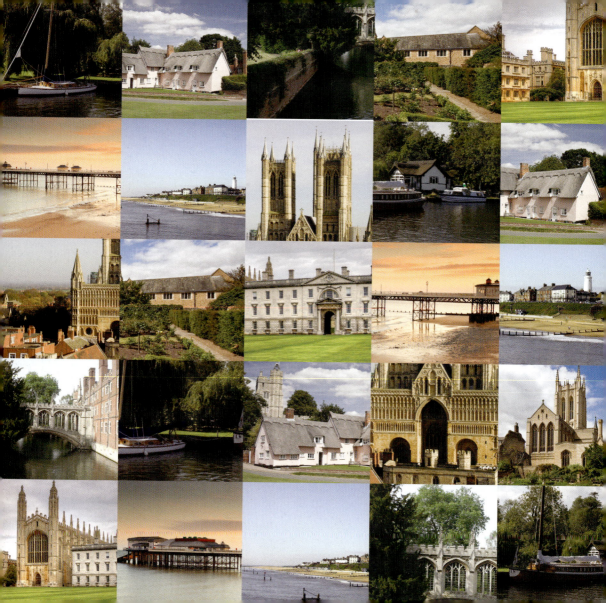

East Anglia

The coastline of East Anglia crumbles defiantly against the relentless barrage of the North Sea, the beaches and coastal villages constantly shifting and evolving.

East Anglia is home to a largely flat landscape that affords incredible panoramic skies. Softened with gently swelling hills, the scenery is predominantly agricultural; patchwork fields of neat, brown, ploughed troughs and furrows, turning to the vibrant green of winter wheat, or soft golden barley and oats. Windmills stand sentry on the skyline, competing with the hundreds of churches that pepper East Anglia, their steeples rising from a misty landscape. Scenes from this rural idyll are reminiscent of seventeenth-century Dutch

landscapes, and the influence of the Dutch here is often apparent, from the Dutch-gabled ends of houses to the drained marshlands of the Fens.

There is a peculiar, ethereal light in East Anglia that is unique to the area. For centuries artists have flocked here to capture that light on canvas; it is not unusual to stumble across tiny, thriving artistic communities settled around pretty village greens.

This is a place of unspoilt beauty that combines rural tranquillity with the architectural splendour of Norwich Cathedral and Cambridge University, and the bustling fishing trade up and down the coastline.

Norfolk Broads

NORFOLK

Right. The Norfolk and Suffolk Broads form the largest protected wetland in Britain, and are an area of outstanding natural beauty. The rivers, lakes, marshes and fens of these areas are home to a wide range of wildlife and birds rarely spotted elsewhere. Years ago the Broads were part of an important transport system, forming a web across East Anglia; now, however, they are a top destination for boating enthusiasts, drawn by the tranquil landscape and beautiful, unique light of this part of the country.

Bridge of Sighs

CAMBRIDGESHIRE

Next page. What better way to spend a lazy day in the Cambridge sun than punting on the scenic River Cam. Here the New Bridge, also known as the Bridge of Sighs, links the Third Court and New Court of St John's College. The bridge was built in 1831 by Henry Hutchinson and follows the style of the sixteenth-century Bridge of Sighs in Venice. The Venetian bridge housed prisoners, but here the barred windows are to prevent students getting in during the night, not prisoners getting out!

King's College Chapel
CAMBRIDGESHIRE

Right. Uplifting and inspiring, King's College Chapel is perhaps the best example of perpendicular architecture in Britain. The magnificent, soaring stone roof with fan tracery cannot fail to make an impact on all who see it; the sheer scale of human endeavour involved in building this was enormous. The chapel was begun by Henry VI in 1446, but work stopped during the Wars of the Roses, and it was not finally finished until 1515. Among other treasures, the chapel houses *The Adoration of The Magi* by Paul Rubens.

Cavendish Village Green
SUFFOLK

Next page. Time slows down in Suffolk; the air is fresh, the scenery glorious and the traditional English villages are at their most lovely. Pretty houses nestle round the billiard-table green, the church of St Mary casting her benign shadow. The small village of Cavendish is one of many similar treasures to be found in Suffolk. Setting off on a rural road, one comes across any number of 'secret' villages, at the heart of which there is almost always a village green, and generally a good pub!

Southwold
SUFFOLK

Right. This small town sits on a cliff above the North Sea; the white lighthouse soars into the sky, a beacon of guidance and direction. The lighthouse was built in the 1880s and stands at just over 30 metres tall. Southwold is a charming place, from her picturesque streets to the immaculate village greens. The brightly painted beach huts and attractive beaches make Southwold one of the most popular coastal resorts, but the town still retains much of its original, traditional character.

Bury Abbey and Cathedral
SUFFOLK

Next page. There was already a monastery here when, in 869, King Edmund of East Anglia was laid to rest. Killed by pagan Vikings, he had died a martyr for his faith; he was canonized as St Edmund not long after. His murderers had decapitated him, it was said, and thrown his head into a deep thicket, but it had called out to his Christian followers till they had found it. Such stories inspired the construction of a great abbey here in the eleventh century; the cathedral came later, built on the site of the abbey church.

South-East England

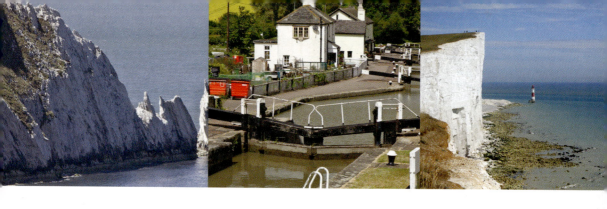

The counties of the South-East cover a vast corner of England, from the lively eastern coastline of Essex, inland to the chalky Chiltern Hills of Buckinghamshire and the windblown Berkshire Downs, and south to the glorious cliffs and beaches of Hampshire, Sussex and Kent.

Autumn sees the dense beech trees of Buckinghamshire afire with gold and russet red, the Thames snaking through the landscape and into Berkshire, home to Windsor Castle and the magnificent Order of the Garter ceremony. To the south lies Hampshire with her seafaring

traditions, and to the east is Surrey in her manicured perfection. The elegant Surrey homes give way to the grandiose splendour of Sussex – land of sheep and the skylark – leading to the high chalk cliffs of the south coast. Kent, the garden county, sits on the south-east tip of England, and boasts one of the most fertile and productive stretches of farmland. Famous for her fruit-growing and cultivation of hops, Kent's landscape is punctuated by unique, conical oast houses. The enchanting countryside is just part of the appeal of the South-East, for this is also an area full of delightful villages and bustling, historic towns.

Ivinghoe Beacon
BUCKINGHAMSHIRE

Right. It is hard to believe the Chiltern Hills lie just a few miles north-west of London; their breathtaking beauty, green, rolling hills, valleys, beech woods and wildlife are a nature lover's paradise. The great Ivinghoe Beacon is majestic in the background here. This late Bronze-Age fort sits on one of the highest hills in the Chilterns, and has commanding views across the countryside. It is the oldest such fort, and sits at the head of the Icknield Way, a Roman thoroughfare stretching to East Anglia.

Grand Union Canal
BUCKINGHAMSHIRE

Next page. Prior to the massive development of road transport during the 1950s, Britain's canals were vital to its industrial evolution. The Grand Junction Canal, later called the Grand Union Canal in the 1930s, was the main link between London and the rest of the British canal system, the canals forming a web of watery thoroughfares from one end of the country to the other. Today the canals are primarily used for pleasure; the appeal of gliding gently in a long boat has become part of the fabric of Britain's tourist trade.

Medmenham Abbey
BUCKINGHAMSHIRE

Right. The picturesque tranquillity of this scene is far-removed from the lively, exotic and colourful past that this area has known. The original abbey was home to Cistercian monks, known for their frugal and penitent life. By the eighteenth century, the abbey was privately owned and had become the meeting place for the Hell Fire Club – a high-class brothel and the scene of lascivious goings-on. Shielded from the road, the abbey sat above a series of underground caves: the perfect location for undisturbed bad behaviour!

Knebworth House
HERTFORDSHIRE

Next page. Opulent and splendid, Knebworth House is a visual delight and never more so than on a summer day when the gardens are in full bloom. The house was begun in 1492 by Sir Robert Lytton, and has remained in the Lytton family ever since. In 1812 part of the building was destroyed, although the grand Tudor Hall survived. In 1843 the first Lord Lytton stamped the exterior with the Gothic style; today the house is a riot of Gothic excess, from its turrets to its gargoyles.

River Stour
ESSEX

Right. The rural delight of such a scene was the inspiration for John Constable, the famous British landscape painter of the early nineteenth century. He was born not far from this spot and grew up along the banks of the River Stour, a landscape of enchantment that remained with him his whole life. The River Stour formed the natural boundary between the kingdoms of Essex and East Anglia in Anglo-Saxon times; now, however, it joins the two counties together through a series of charming bridges.

Balloon Festival
KENT

Next page. The smooth green fields are a perfect backdrop to the bright hot-air balloons as they take off in a riot of colour – brilliant, boiled-sweet hues lifting up and away. What better way to appreciate the beauty of the countryside fully than with a bird's-eye view? Be prepared for an early start though – the best balloon flights catch the early morning hours, as the landscape starts to come to life in preparation for a new day.

Canterbury Cathedral
KENT

Right. The fifteenth-century bell tower dominates the skyline of Canterbury. It is particularly poignant at sunset when the dying sun bathes the building in blood-red light, bringing to mind the fate of Thomas Becket, murdered in the cathedral in 1170. This most holy of places is central to Anglican Christianity in Britain and has one of the oldest histories as a site of Christian worship. For centuries it has been a place of pilgrimage; 'The Pilgrim's Way' is a pre-Roman path linking Winchester to Canterbury.

Leeds Castle
KENT

Next page. Rising majestically from the still waters of its surrounding moat, Leeds Castle glistens in the soft light, appearing unworldly, the fabric of legend and fantasy. Its history, however, is resoundingly real; the castle has been host to a procession of notable occupants from Catherine of Aragon to Elizabeth I. Leeds is sometimes referred to as the most beautiful of British castles, and it is not hard to see why. Enclosed by 500 acres (202 hectares) of stunning parkland and manicured gardens, this is certainly one of Britain's jewels.

White Cliffs of Dover

KENT

Right. Rising imposingly from the sea, the white cliffs of Dover are as memorable and startling as any natural formation. This dramatic landscape feature, where the rolling North Downs fall into the sea in a tumble of brilliant white chalk, stares across the English Channel towards France. Just 21 miles (34 km) away is Calais and the French coastline. Over the centuries the cliffs have been in the frontline of defence, the first port of call for attacking invaders, but today they remain inextricably bound in a sense of nostalgia.

Bluebell Line

SUSSEX

Next page. This shiny engine, no. 178, looks every bit as impressive now as it did when it was first commissioned; a relic of the golden age of steam, when Britain's industries and tourism expanded rapidly, due in large part to improved rail transport. The Bluebell Line was Britain's first preserved, standard-gauge passenger railway and re-opened part of the old London to Brighton and South Coast Railway back in 1960. The trains, carriages and wagons are beautifully preserved and continue to operate on a daily basis.

Beachy Head
SUSSEX

Right. Towering 295 feet (90 m) above the sea, Beachy Head is the highest cliff top on the south-east coast of Britain. It is a dramatic spot, the sea crashing below and sea gulls wheeling above, their screams piercing and far-reaching. The original lighthouse was built on the cliff top and was used until 1899, when it threatened to collapse. The new lighthouse was constructed in 1902 by Sir Thomas Matthews, and sits 541 feet (165 m) seawards from the base of the cliffs.

Brighton Royal Pavilion
SUSSEX

Next page. The Oriental vision of the Royal Pavilion is one of extravagance, opulence and exuberance – it is one of the most unusual and original buildings in Britain. The building was commissioned by George IV and started out in 1783 as a classical house with a Chinese interior. In 1812 John Nash was engaged to overhaul the building, giving it added flair and whimsy. The Pavilion was at the centre of a divided criticism at the time, and has been subjected to equal measures of derision, intrigue and adoration ever since.

Hastings
SUSSEX

Right. As an island, Britain has for a long time had a reputation as a country of fish – the famous English dish of fish and chips is now worldwide fare; however, it never seems as good as when it has been caught and cooked in Britain. Fishing as an industry has suffered recently, but here the brightly coloured fishing boats line the beach, waiting to go to work. Hastings is home to 'The Stade', a fisherman's beach which boasts the largest fishing fleet worked from the beach in the country.

Hampton Court Palace
SURREY

Next page. The magnificent palace was built in 1514 by Cardinal Wolsey and became the favourite country retreat for Henry VIII. It was the scene of court life to excess, and of 500 years of turbulent history. The grounds still echo with the thunder of horses charging in jousting matches, the roar of the crowds and the melancholy sigh of five of Henry's six wives who lived here. During William III's accession in the seventeenth century, Sir Christopher Wren created the Baroque style of the east front.

Winchester Cathedral
HAMPSHIRE

Right. Along with Canterbury, Winchester has been the other major place of pilgrimage for Christians in Britain through the ages. The great Winchester Cathedral, which is the longest in Europe, was begun in 1079 and was built in stages over several hundred years. The massive monument to the indomitable spirit of religion presides over the city that was once the capital of England. There is an air of reassuring permanence to Winchester Cathedral; its vast bulk appears as indestructible and stalwart as the beliefs of its faithful leaders.

Micheldever Cottage
HAMPSHIRE

Next page. There is nothing quite like an English country cottage garden, and this profusion of flowers outside a thatched cottage in Micheldever would seem to capture precisely everything that a cottage garden should be. The patchwork of summer colours and unruly explosion of natural exuberance is the perfect companion to the cottage's old-world charm. The ancient town of Micheldever, dating back to the Saxons and mentioned in the Domesday Book, is at the heart of Hampshire, and is yet another of this county's idyllic spots.

Beaulieu Palace
HAMPSHIRE

Right. The daffodils at Beaulieu zing with colour, heralding the start of a new spring and closing the door on winter. The beautiful Palace House at Beaulieu is a fitting backdrop for such lovely flowers. Nestled in the heart of the New Forest, Beaulieu was originally the gatehouse to the Beaulieu Abbey. Little remains of the Abbey, but the monastic origins of the house can still be felt. The house, which was rebuilt in the Gothic style in 1872, sits in stunning grounds that extend down to the Beaulieu River.

New Forest Ponies
HAMPSHIRE

Next page. William the Conqueror created the New Forest in 1079 to serve as a royal hunting ground, primarily of deer. The beautiful wilderness is home to many different species of trees and plants, as well as wildlife. It is a unique area of historical importance in Britain, and still retains many of the rural practices laid down by the crown in medieval times. One of the most significant of these is the right of the 'commoners' to graze their ponies, cattle, pigs and donkeys across the New Forest acreage.

HMS *Victory*
HAMPSHIRE

Right. As majestic now as she was when she rode the high seas, the HMS *Victory* sits resplendent in Portsmouth's Royal Navy Dockyards. She is the world's oldest commissioned warship, and is most famous as being Nelson's flagship during the Battle of Trafalgar. She was retired from active duty in 1812, after 32 years of heroic efforts in the front line of Britain's navy, and was anchored in Portsmouth harbour for the next 110 years. In 1922 she was moved to a dry dock and carefully restored.

Cowes Week
ISLE OF WIGHT

Next page. Sails bowing into the wind, vibrant boats skim across the smooth surface of the English Channel, competing in the world's most exclusive sailing regatta. The bright sails, set against the surprisingly exotic blue of the Channel, makes this a visual delight. The annual Cowes Week is the Grand National of sailing; a week-long festival of races, parties, shopping, fireworks and more. The event has a historic tradition, having started in 1826, and now sees over 1,000 boats competing.

The Needles
ISLE OF WIGHT

Right. The mysterious Needles, the tailbone of a long chalk ridge that runs the length of the Isle of Wight, poke through the water's surface. They appear part rock, part something magical, as if teetering on the point of diving back down below the waves. The chalk stacks and the red and white lighthouse, warning ships with its foghorn, are arguably the most iconic images of the Isle of Wight. A nearby chairlift ride is a great way to view this stunning landmark, offering up a spectacular view.

Windsor Castle
BERKSHIRE

Next page. Windsor Castle is the magnificent castle around which the town of Windsor has grown. It is the largest and most stunning of castles in England and has the honour of being the Royal Family's favourite home. History, tradition, pomp and splendour all play a part in the fabric of Windsor, and it is here that the compelling Order of the Garter Ceremony takes place. Dating back to medieval times of honour and chivalry, this pageant of colour and traditional festivity is a great attraction for visitors and locals alike.

London

Two thousand years of history are caught up amongst London's streets and buildings, the pavements echoing with the memory of her past and resounding with intensity as she heads towards the future.

London is the ultimate melting pot of cosmopolitan life; she is the city that offers everything. Founded around AD 43 by the Romans, the original settlement grew in the area now known as the City's Square Mile. From early beginnings London evolved into a powerhouse, and continues to be the beating heart of Britain's commerce and industry, retail,

tourism and entertainment. Growing organically around the River Thames, London is full of surprising, twisting streets, tiny rows of mews houses and urban vistas. Each step brings a new view: a church by Sir Christopher Wren, a square, a park, a statue, a modern glittering office building, a gently sweeping crescent of elegant Regency houses. The capital is home to some of the greatest art galleries, museums, shops and theatres in the world. It is a city of contrasts, from the stately Houses of Parliament to the raucous Trafalgar Square, the energy of the Millenium Dome (The O_2), to the tranquillity of a stroll through St James's Park.

London Eye and Big Ben

Right. Framed in a night sky of glowing red, Big Ben appears within the great London Eye, a juxtaposition of old and new, each as aesthetically pleasing as the other. This beautiful sunset view blocks out the noise and bustle of London, leaving only a landscape of infinite calm. The London Eye, created as a millennium landmark, slowly revolves and offers visitors views of up to 25 miles (40 km) across some of London's greatest buildings, and as far as Windsor Castle in the distance.

Big Ben and Houses of Parliament

Next page. The stately Gothic grace of the Houses of Parliament was created between 1840 and 1860 by Sir Charles Barry and A.W. Pugin, who built this 'new' building on the site of the former royal residence; this is one of the most universally recognised buildings in Britain. Jostled up to the Houses of Parliament stands Big Ben, the statuesque clock tower that rings melodically across London. Big Ben is actually the name of the largest bell in the tower, which was cast in 1858.

Trooping the Colour, Horse Guards

Right. Lined up in bright rows of ruby red, the troops from the Household Division take part in the traditional Trooping the Colour, a ceremony that marks the Queen's official birthday. This ceremony has been used to honour the sovereign's birthday since 1748, and is just one of many richly historic traditions for which Britain is famous. The event is held on Horse Guards Parade, Whitehall; during Trooping the Colour the Queen is given a royal salute and she inspects the troops before they march past her.

Trafalgar Square

Next page. The towering Norwegian Spruce Christmas tree is a beacon of fairy lights, lending a magical feel to an already magical place – Trafalgar Square at night in the run up to Christmas. The tree has been donated every year since 1947 by the city of Oslo in Norway to the City of Westminster, as a token of appreciation for Britain's friendship during the Second World War. Seen here, the towering tree reflects the steeple of St Martin-in-the-Fields, both graceful and beautifully lit.

St James's Park

Right. Such a peaceful scene could be deep in the heart of the country, but instead it is St James's Park, another of London's oases of green and tranquillity. This is one of the oldest of London's parks, and also one of the smallest. It has a very royal location, sitting as it does between three palaces: Buckingham Palace, St James's Palace, and Westminster. The park dates back to the thirteenth century, but it was Charles II who formally landscaped the space and opened it to the public.

Buckingham Palace

Next page. A horizontal sweep of classical grandeur set behind a slash of red and purple – spring is perhaps the best time of year to see this stately palace. Buckingham Palace has been the main royal residence since Queen Victoria moved here in 1837. Prior to that, the palace had relatively humble beginnings, originally being a town house for the Duke of Buckingham. John Nash created the palace in 1820 and it was later remodelled by Edward Blore. The Classical façade was added in 1913 by Sir Aston Webb.

St Paul's Cathedral

Right. The open-top bus tour is one of the capital's best-loved tourist attractions, and here the bus passes one of the most significant of London sights. The City of London has been watched over by a St Paul's Cathedral since AD 604; the current one was built between 1675 and 1710 by Sir Christopher Wren, following the destruction of the previous cathedral during the Great Fire of London. St Paul's is the scene of most major commemorative events in the country, from royal weddings to funerals and remembrance services.

City of London from Waterloo Bridge

Next page. One of the most stunning visual aspects to London is the combination of old and new buildings; the coupling of modern skyscrapers with historic churches, the one a temple to commerce, the other to religion. The skyline of the city is a case in point. The dome of St Paul's Cathedral, built by Sir Christopher Wren, sits resplendent amongst shining towers of glass and steel. The view from Waterloo Bridge provides one of the most captivating vistas of the City of London, especially on a fine, sunny day.

City of London from Tower Bridge

Right. In the heart of London lies the City, one square mile (2.6 square km) and domicile to the nation's high finance. The buildings are the same eclectic mix of old and new that London is so famous for, although the modern skyscrapers now dominate the skyline. This is where London began; the site of the original Londinium built within the second-century Roman walls. The Tower of London, grand in the distance and the scene of much bloodshed, looks towards the elegant 'Gherkin', a stunning feat of modern engineering.

Tower of London

Next page. This fortress has a history stretching back to William the Conqueror who built the great White Tower in around 1097. During the thirteenth century the White Tower was fortified with two lines of defensive walls and the Royal Mint was moved there, safe behind the thick walls. The Tower was used as a palace, fortress and prison, holding captive such royals as Anne Boleyn, Lady Jane Grey and the Duke of Monmouth, before they were executed in the centre of the complex on Tower Green.

Millennium Dome

Right. The ethereal glow of the Millennium Dome by night lends the structure an unearthly, phantasmagoric appeal. Quite unlike anything else built before, the Dome appears to hover above the ground, caught in a transitory place – a quality that in part reflects the chequered history and future of this huge structure. Unveiled for the millennium, the Dome failed to attract the crowds, cost millions of pounds, and closed one year later. It is now home to a large entertainment district known as The O_2, housing an indoor arena, music club, cinema, exhibition space, piazzas and several bars and restaurants.

Thames Flood Barrier

Next page. One could be forgiven for mistaking the Thames Flood Barrier for a piece of modern sculptural art; great shining steel pods rearing up from the water like a series of impressive sentries. The flood barrier is actually an extraordinary piece of engineering, a system of vast steel gates that can be raised in the event of an emergency. Continual threat of flooding along the Thames Estuary expedited the building of the flood barrier, and it was finally unveiled in 1982 by Queen Elizabeth II.

South-West England

From the rugged, untamed coastlines of Cornwall and Devon to the enigmatic Salisbury Plain in Wiltshire, the unsurpassable elegance of the historic town of Bath in Avon to the towering cliffs and gorges of Somerset and the wild heathlands of Thomas Hardy country in Dorset, the South-West of England holds an infinite and indefinable appeal.

It is an area inextricably bound with legend and mystery, the shadow of King Arthur and his knights woven into the very fabric of Cornish life and landscape. The romantically picturesque moorlands of Devon, characterised by Dartmoor's desolate beauty, are stage indeed for great plays of the imagination. Neighbouring Somerset is rich

in lush green pastures, a county of farmers and fishermen; in nearby Avon is the ancient town of Bath. Across Dorset, chalk hills undulate gently, rolling into the huge chalk cliffs stretching from Lyme Regis to Burton Bradstock. Small and lovely villages typify Dorset's rural charm, scattered amongst large tracts of productive dairy farmland that cross into Wiltshire.

Yet again a rich tapestry of contrasts, the South-West remains breathtakingly beautiful and largely unspoilt; mysterious, wild, charming and exhilarating, the South-West of England is a destination to inspire all the senses.

Castle Combe
WILTSHIRE

Right. Set into the beautiful Cotswold Hills, Castle Combe is one of the prettiest English villages. The By Brook wends its way sleepily past a row of old weavers' cottages, their mellow stone and steeply pitched roofs typical of Cotswold buildings. Cloth-weaving was the main industry here, and the regular wool market was held at the fifteenth-century market cross near the packhorse bridge. St Andrew's church and tower was built in 1434 at the expense of the local weavers, and is full of stone and wood decoration.

White Horse
WILTSHIRE

Next page. Hillside figures are always startling; gleaming white and in massive proportions, they cannot fail to stir the senses. The Westbury White Horse (also known as the Bratton White Horse) is no exception. It is situated close to the Iron Age hill fort Bratton Camp and it also holds the honour of being the oldest of the white horses in Wiltshire, first being referenced in a document dated to 1742. Its exact origins are unknown, but one theory is that it was created to commemorate the victory of King Alfred at the Battle of Ethandun in AD 878.

Salisbury Cathedral
WILTSHIRE

Right. The magnificent early English Gothic building of Salisbury Cathedral is one of the finest surviving examples of this type of architecture. The soaring verticality of the building and fine sculptural work cannot fail to uplift a weary soul. The cathedral is unique because it was conceived and built as a single unit, unlike almost every other building of this size. Work began in 1220 and the cathedral was completed in an extraordinarily fast 60 years. Only the spire, the tallest in England, was added separately in 1334.

Stonehenge
WILTSHIRE

Next page. Wide-open Salisbury Plain exudes a sense of mystery; the presence of an ancient history is tangible here, alive still, but not understood. Stonehenge sits at the heart of the plain – silent, brooding stones, monuments to something beyond our reach. This is the best preserved of the Bronze-Age sites, a structure built over thousands of years, with an almost incomprehensible effort of sheer manpower and dedication. This ancient temple continues to inspire all those who see it, moved by the inexplicable sense of part elation, part fear.

Longleat House
WILTSHIRE

Right. Longleat House was started in 1568 by Sir John Thynne and is a fine example of an early Renaissance home. The stately building is set in 900 acres (364 hectares) of grounds, the gardens of which were laid out by the famous landscaper Capability Brown. The house is as famous for its ornate ceilings and abundant use of gilt as it is for its eccentric owner, the 7th Marquess of Bath. Longleat also houses a particularly impressive library, which is home to the 'First Folio' of William Shakespeare's plays.

Clifton Suspension Bridge
AVON

Next page. Soaring across the spectacular Avon Gorge in Bristol is the Clifton Suspension Bridge, itself almost as dramatic as the limestone cliffs that it joins. The bridge was begun in 1831, built to the designs of Isambard Kingdom Brunel – amazingly it was his first major commission. The project suffered from financial and political hindrances and was abandoned, half-built, in 1843. Brunel died unexpectedly, and in 1853 work resumed on the bridge – now it was to be his memorial. Today it remains magnificent, modern beyond its time and unremittingly awe-inspiring.

West Doors of Bath Abbey
AVON

Right. The spectacular Bath Abbey sits right at the heart of Bath and on the site of two previous churches. The first dated from AD 757 but was destroyed in 1066; a second Norman church replaced it, but by the end of the fifteenth century this too was in ruins. The present abbey was begun in 1499, and is one of the last great medieval abbeys. The West Front is captivating and has carved angels climbing up and down ladders on each of the turrets flanking the window.

Roman Baths
AVON

Next page. Seen by night, the Roman Baths in Bath are a haunting place of ethereal beauty, the soft lights reflected in the flat, still surface of a seemingly bottomless pool. These are the best-preserved Roman remains in Britain, and demonstrate just how advanced the Romans were with technology. Adjacent to the baths is the Georgian Pump Room, a lovely, Neoclassical room of great sophistication, where water was drawn for drinking. The baths were central to society in Roman times, and retained their position of importance for centuries.

Royal Crescent

AVON

Right. Across a glorious profusion of colour, the elegant façade of the Royal Crescent is just visible. Bath is one of the finest Georgian towns and retains much of its original character. The Royal Crescent, beautifully positioned against the formal brilliance of Victoria Park, was built to the designs of John Wood the Younger between 1767 and 1774. It is a masterpiece of the best architecture and decoration of the time, and was built to accommodate wealthy visitors to the town. Number One, Royal Crescent is now home to the Bath Preservation Trust.

Pulteney Bridge

AVON

Next page. The extraordinary Pulteney Bridge, designed by Robert Adam in 1770, is one of only four bridges in the world to house shops, and clearly shows its debt to the Ponte Vecchio in Florence and Ponte di Rialto in Venice. The bridge was commissioned by the entrepreneurial William Pulteney to join Bath with an area ripe for development on the opposite side of the river. Over the years, the bridge was greatly changed with detrimental effect, but in 1975 it was thoroughly restored and remains one of Bath's greatest treasures.

Cheddar Gorge
SOMERSET

Right. Deep in Somerset lies one of the most spectacular natural wonders of Britain, the Cheddar Gorge. Great limestone cliffs soar to an incredible 450 feet (137 m) above sea level, making them the highest cliffs in the country. Once a great river would have cut this swathe through the limestone; now the river runs underground leaving its legacy of cliffs and caves behind. This is an ancient place, the many caves having offered shelter to early man. Now they are home to the rare horseshoe bat and many species of birds.

Glastonbury Abbey
SOMERSET

Next page. Steeped in legend and mystery, Glastonbury Abbey is reputed to be the final resting place of King Arthur and Queen Guinevere; Arthur's spirit still roams the ruins. This is believed to be the site of the earliest Christian church in Britain, and dates back to the seventh century, although the remains are mostly Norman. The abbey became one of the most powerful in the land until Henry VIII hanged the abbot in 1539 and destroyed many of the buildings, using the stone for building elsewhere.

Wells Cathedral
SOMERSET

Right. Wells grew around the natural springs, deemed to have healing powers, that are now in the grounds of Bishop's Palace. A church was built near the wells in AD 705 and the present cathedral was then built on this site from 1180. Wells Cathedral is one of the most impressive cathedrals in Britain, and the west front with its carved statues is the building's crowning glory. The façade was built between 1209 and 1250, and 300 of the original, over-life-size medieval statues have survived.

Porlock Bay
SOMERSET

Next page. The open spaces of Exmoor tumble down towards Porlock Bay in a blaze of purple and yellow, to join the sea of brilliant blue. On a fine summer's day, with just a puff of wind to chivvy the clouds across the sky, the call of seagulls and a warm sun – this is a scene of astonishing beauty. Behind the bay sits an inland salt marsh, a private paradise for a number of unusual wading birds and wildfowl, and a stop-off for little egrets, spoonbills and marsh harriers as they wheel through.

Durdle Door
DORSET

Right. To the east of Dorset lies Bournemouth and to the west Weymouth, but in between can be found some of the most exciting coastline on the south coast. Here the Chaldon Downs end abruptly in white cliffs, which in turn shelter smooth, sandy beaches that brace the ultramarine blue of the sea on a clear day. Durdle Door is a natural archway of Purbeck limestone that juts out into the sea, forming the eastern end of Durdle Door Cove. The white chalk headland, Bats Head, marks the western point of the cove.

Watermouth Cove
DEVON

Next page. Devon's coastline scenes, from the southern point of Welcombe near the Cornish border up to Trentishoe on the north coast, are some of the most wild and ruggedly beautiful to be found in Britain. This is the coast of crashing waves, huge rocks and jutting headlands, so Watermouth Cove forms a peaceful respite. Here the sea is smooth, the beaches shingle and attractive. The nearby small town of Ilfracombe is a popular resort and offers all kinds of boat trips, fishing and golfing for the relaxed holidaymaker.

Combestone Tor
DEVON

Right. The open wilderness of Dartmoor is one of desolate beauty and rough appeal – it offers some of the best horseback riding and hiking in the country, and is home to a wide range of wildlife. Scattered across Dartmoor are a series of tors, impressive rock towers of many layers. One could be forgiven for assuming they are manmade, such is their precisely stacked appearance. Actually they are natural formations, granite rock piles that have been eroded over the centuries by the harsh climate of the open landscape.

Clovelly Harbour
DEVON

Next page. The small village of Clovelly sits in a narrow passage of land between two steep cliffs on the site of an ancient settlement. The village is mentioned in the Domesday Book, but was probably first established by the Saxons. This is a quaint fishing village that has more recently benefited from the tourist industry. Part of Clovelly's appeal lies in its beautiful cottages, flowers and working harbour, but it is also only open to pedestrians – all cars are banned – and this makes it a quiet corner of tranquillity.

Bedruthan Steps
CORNWALL

Right. Cornwall – land of sea, sun and fantastic scenery. The coastline is picturesque in its essence; golden, sandy beaches, black headlands, blue seas and wild flowers. It is an area of legend and mystery, the fairytale landscape adding to the unique charm of this most southerly part of Britain. This scene is typical of Cornwall's coastline; the great granite rocks peppered across the bay are the Bedruthan Steps, allegedly created by the giant Bedruthan to traverse from one end of the bay to the other.

Wheal Coates Old Engine House
CORNWALL

Next page. Standing stark against the sky, the ruins of the Wheal Coates Engine House at first glance appear religious, abandoned from an ancient site of Christianity. Their history is far less civilized. These buildings, halfway down the cliffs just north of the pretty cove of Chapel Porth, housed the engines used to pump water out of the sunken mine shafts. Tin mining was big business here in the nineteenth century; however, conditions were poor and loss of life was a common occurrence.

The Eden Project
CORNWALL

Right. All the glories of an English garden and, bubbling up behind it, plastic domes housing exotic ecosystems or 'biomes'. Here, in the Cornish countryside, are a tiny tropical rainforest and a little corner of the Mediterranean, with grape vines and olive trees; an outdoor biome brings together plants from temperate climates. The Eden Project was created in what was formerly a china clay pit: it opened in the spring of 2001. It was conceived, not just as an educational facility, but as a bold experiment in ecology, vital to our understanding of the natural world.

Polperro Harbour
CORNWALL

Next page. This old fishing village is now a popular destination for holidaymakers, drawn to the pretty, lime-washed houses and slow pace of life. Polperro is everything that a traditional Cornish fishing village typifies: quaint buildings surrounding a small harbour sheltered by two sea walls, narrow cobbled streets and the whispers of smugglers' ghosts echoing through the buildings. Cornwall's coast is famous for the tales of smugglers, their triumphs and their demise, and Polperro is home to her fair share of their stories.

Godrevy Lighthouse
CORNWALL

Right. In the far west of Cornwall is St Ives, a picturesque town of cobbled streets, lovely buildings and sandy beaches. Off the coast of St Ives, situated on a small island, is the Godrevy Lighthouse, standing a lonely watch over the Stones, a treacherous reef stretching for 1½ miles (2.4 km). This was the scene of the devastating shipwreck of the *Nile*, a passenger steamer, in 1854 – all lives were lost. Godrevy was also the inspiration for Virginia Woolf's novel *To The Lighthouse*.

Land's End
CORNWALL

Next page. This is the most westerly point of Britain, separated from the Scilly Isles and the coast of America by miles and miles of sea. It is a place of legend, mystery and folklore; the landscape inspiring, evocative and beautiful. Here the great Penwith Peninsular falls into the sea in a mass of rock. The sun sets, one last dying orange flare dropping into the sea and leaving this place of infinite magic, great natural sculptures of granite holding the secrets of times gone by.

Acknowledgements

Biographies

Tamsin Pickeral graduated from Reading University with an honours degree in History of Art and Architecture. Following further studying in Italy, the author turned her attentions to adventure. She has travelled extensively, and has recently returned to Britain having spent the last nine years living on a cattle ranch in the US. Prior to that she lived in Italy, and has journeyed through most of Europe and across Australia. Despite her wanderlust it is Britain that she keeps returning to, finding it an endless source of inspiration for her books. When not exploring the British countryside, the author divides her time between her beloved horses and writing.

Michael Kerrigan lives in Edinburgh, where he writes regularly for the *Scotsman* newspaper. He is a book reviewer for *The Times Literary Supplement* and the *Guardian*, London. As an author, he has published extensively on both British and world history and prehistory. He has been a contributor to Flame Tree's *World History* and *Irish History* as well as to *The Times Encyclopaedia of World Religion* (2001). His contributions to this book can be found on the following pages: 24(b), 36, 56(b), 72(b), 84(t), 122(b), 246(t).

Picture Credits

Courtesy of/© Shutterstock.com and the following contributors: Chris Frost 21; Ian McDonald 22–23; Steve Allen 25; Richard Bowden 26–27; Rosli Othman 29; KevinTate 30–31; Alastair Wallace 33; Daniel J. Rao 34–35; Atlaspix 37; sjm1 38–39; Shanna Hyatt 42–43; GrahamMoore999 49; Steve Buckley 50–51; albinoni 53; Mike Charles 54–55, 244–45; Stephen Gibson 57; Gordon Bell 58–59, 112–13; Semmick Photo 61; kenny1 62–63; Chris Green 66–67; David Hughes 73; WDG Photo 77; Dave Massey 78–79; Steve Heap 81; Arena Photo UK 82–83, 93; Matthew Dixon 85; stocker1970 101, 215, 216–17, 252–53; David Steele 90–91; Christopher Day 94–95; Chris Pole 97; Andrei Nekrassov 102–03; Artur Bogacki 111; Jason Saunders 116–17; Hipgnosis 119; Len Green 123; Tom Gowanlock 124–25; Gordon Bell 132–33; Pawel Kowalczyk 143; Benson HE 144–45; John Hemmings 147; Philip Bird LRPS CPAGB 148–49; Dmitry Naumov 152–53; Milan Gonda 155; Paul Cummings 159; Henk Hennuin 164–65; Darren Baker 168–69; Stephen Clarke 171; Bikeworldtravel 179; Emma manners 183; Elena Elisseeva 187; Simon James 188–89; QQ7 192–93; timages 195; mikecphoto 199; JeniFoto 207 , 219, 220–21; Alan Jeffery 208–09; Bertl123 211; MPanchenko 212–13; ian woolcock 224–25, 236–37, 243; Fulcanelli 228–29; Richard Melichar 231; DavidYoung 232–33; Gail Johnson 235; Helen Hotson 239; Undivided 240–41; Francesco Carucci 247; Rolf E. Staerk 248–49; Paul Nash 251.

Courtesy of/© iStock and the following contributors: Arpad Benedek 41; George-Standen 65; fotoVoyager 98–99; Linda Steward 115; kbwills 139; mirrormere 151; Lillasam 156–57; PKM1 167; villorejo 172–73; Deejpilot 180–81; shanneong 184–85; Maui01 191; ssupple1 196–97; asmithers 200–01; jeffthemongoose 223; George-Standen 227.

Courtesy of/© Getty and the following contributors: jimennisphotography.co.uk 74–75; Joe Cornish 86–87; James Osmond 89; David Toase 105; Robin Bush 120–21, 131; De Agostini/W. Buss 136–37; VisitBritain/Pawel Libera 140–41; Andy Williams 163.

Courtesy of/© Superstock and the following contributor: Travel Library Limited 135, 160–61.

Index